Aura

How to See Auras in 7 Easy Steps

By Mia Rose

© Copyright 2015 by Mia Rose- All rights reserved.

This document is geared towards providing exact and reliable information in regards to the topic and issue covered. The publication is sold with the idea that the publisher is not required to render accounting, officially permitted, or otherwise, qualified services. If advice is necessary, legal or professional, a practiced individual in the profession should be ordered.

- From a Declaration of Principles which was accepted and approved equally by a Committee of the American Bar Association and a Committee of Publishers and Associations.

In no way is it legal to reproduce, duplicate, or transmit any part of this document in either electronic means or in printed format. Recording of this publication is strictly prohibited and any storage of this document is not allowed unless with written permission from the publisher. All rights reserved.

The information provided herein is stated to be truthful and consistent, in that any liability, in terms of inattention or otherwise, by any usage or abuse of any policies, processes, or directions contained within is the solitary and utter responsibility of the recipient reader. Under no circumstances will any legal responsibility or blame be held against the publisher for any reparation, damages, or monetary loss due to the information herein, either directly or indirectly.

Respective authors own all copyrights not held by the publisher.

The information herein is offered for informational purposes solely, and is universal as so. The presentation of the information is without contract or any type of guarantee assurance.

The trademarks that are used are without any consent, and the publication of the trademark is without permission or backing by the trademark owner. All trademarks and brands within this book are for clarifying purposes only and are the owned by the owners themselves, not affiliated with this document.

Table of Contents

Introduction

Chapter 1

All about Auras

    What is An Aura?

    Science and Auras

    Can It Be Seen?

    Science and Spirituality, Why all the Conflict?

    A New Approach

    Auras, the Future and You

    How to Use This Book

Chapter 2

Seeing Auras: Getting Started

    Step 1: Setting the Scene

    Step 2. Losing Focus and Staying Concentrated

        Blinking

        Opening the Third Eye or Brow Chakra

        The First Aura

    Congratulations

Chapter 3

The Next Steps; Broadening Your Skills

    Step 3: Mixing Things Up

    Step 4: Your First Living Aura

    Step 5 – Big Plants!

Step Six: Animal Magnetism

Step 7: The Big One

    The Human Guinea Pig

    Color Correspondences

Finally

Conclusion

Preview of Reiki for Beginners

Check Out My Other Books

About the Author

Introduction

I want to thank you and congratulate you for downloading the book, *"How To See Auras; In 7 Easy Steps"*.

This book contains proven steps and strategies on how to learn to see Auras.

The art of seeing Auras is an ancient skill but it is one that is possible for anybody to learn. Viewing Auras, in fact, seems to be a natural talent that we all possess but is one that we rarely learn from childhood in modern Western countries. This book takes you through seven very simple steps which will teach you to see Auras or yourself. If you've ever wondered if Auras are "real", then this book will hold the answers for you!

Thanks again for downloading this book, I hope you enjoy it!

Chapter 1
All about Auras

References to Auras can be found in literature and art dating back to at least the culture of Ancient Egypt and in just about every tradition in the world. From Chinese religious and spiritual traditions, it is defined as energy called "Chi" to the Vedic traditions of India where it is called "prana". Early (and modern) Christian imagery is littered with depictions of Christ, the Virgin Mary and the Saints surrounded by a halo of light. Many modern spiritual movements including several New Age movements recognize the existence of the Aura. Today, however, scientists remain skeptical about the concept.

What is An Aura?

An aura is believed to be a light radiating from all things; from plants, animals, humans, rocks and every other object you can imagine. In many traditions the color and state of the aura are said to represent the physical, emotional and spiritual state of the individual concerned. Ancient traditions viewed the radiation emanating from an individual to be representative of the "life force" of the universe that fills, according to these traditions, everything in creation. Many modern traditions have taken up this theory and the aura is linked largely to concepts of a spiritual nature but is also found commonly in many healing traditions, both ancient and modern.

Science and Auras

In scientific terms energy is emitted from all objects at some level. Radiation from the Sun, for example, can be seen in terms of light and heat and it extends far beyond the physical body of our local star. On a more down to earth level there is little argument in science that objects emit "radiation" in one form or another. Science would agree that as humans we emit "radiation", in terms of energy and heat, but scientist in general do not agree that this energy can be seen, or visualized, as an aura. However, there are some scientific facts which can link ancient understanding of auras and their link to our health.

Electrical reactions within our body are a scientific fact. The heart gives off electrical impulses and localized magnetic fields are generated around our heads which are caused by very small electrical currents in our brains. Although we may not realize it we are all, just a little, powered by electricity! Many of those who argue in support of auras suggest that the colored light that surrounds the body is simply radiation that is the result of these processes. They also argue that illness in any form in the body can disrupt its normal functions and in turn disrupt this energy field. In other animals and plants the same holds true and in even in non-human objects and apparently lifeless objects energy is (by the nature of the universe) present and can create small readings in terms of radiation. The main area of contention between those who support auras and scientific understanding of the energy radiating from and around our bodies is simply that it cannot be "seen".

Can It Be Seen?

For those interested in auras, one area of study is of extreme interest. Kirlian Photography has demonstrated that by placing a subject directly onto film, or a photographic plate, and passing a small electrical current through it an image of the apparent aura can be captured. The technique developed by Semyon Kirlian in the 1950s is still contentious but the images themselves offer an outstandingly beautiful and tantalizing glimpse into the real nature of auras. Experiments conducted by Kirlian and his wife clearly demonstrate a link between health and vitality and their opposites. Images of leaves plucked from both healthy and diseased plants showed remarkable differences in the level of energy emitted by the corona or aura of the leaf.

Science and Spirituality, Why all the Conflict?

Science and spiritual traditions both seek to explain, explore and understand the universe around us. For centuries the disciplines were linked but, in the West at least, this has not been true for many centuries. The conflict between scientific understanding and spiritual understanding has been a long one, a complex one and at times a very bitter one. While in many cultures science, medicine and spirituality have all combined to provide a single frame of reference in the search for knowledge and enlightenment, in the West by the Middle Ages the different disciplines had begun to take different paths. This divergence inevitably led to conflict; by the 17th century the church and science were polarized in their understanding of the world around us. Galileo (1564

– 1642) considered today to be the father of several major scientific disciplines, including astronomy, physics and modern science in general, was convicted of heresy and spent the last nine years of his life under house arrest as a result. This was just the start of things for the "war" between modern science and Western spiritual traditions. After skirmishes throughout the Enlightenment and prolonged battles in the Victorian era, modern Western science and medicine seemed to have won the day.

A New Approach

However, the victory has been far from complete. As the world has changed in the last century Eastern and Western cultures have become more accessible to each other and a resurgence in interest in "forgotten" elements of spirituality has developed. In the East, the split between medical, scientific and spiritual knowledge has not been so clear cut. Healing methods in many Eastern traditions look at dealing with the whole body and focus on prevention rather than cure. The West had, until recently, taken a different stance. In many traditions, established practices such as herbal medicine and meditation are now being recognized as having real, scientifically founded beneficial effects. Gradually, an acceptance is growing amongst medical authorities and institutions in the West of the science behind some of the beliefs and practices. This is not to say that *all* ancient beliefs are based on scientific fact but simply that we are still to discover much about ourselves and the universe we occupy and science is accepting it may not have all the answers, just yet! In the case of auras, this has yet to happen but it may be that as scientists and society in the West begin to explore more deeply the subject, some proof may emerge that the physical, emotional state of an individual can be read by examining the state of the energy radiating from that person.

Auras, the Future and You

Until that point it is down to the individuals who practice the study of auras to contribute to our understanding of the subject and to help us discover their true nature. Auras appear as visible light to those who see them – although many people believe that the light itself may just be a visual representation constructed by the brain to interpret our reactions to physical responses to the energy field radiating from the body (or object). While modern science may, as yet, dismiss the concept of seeing auras, the good news is that traditions which accept the phenomenon believe that all of us are capable of viewing auras. Some people seem to be able to do so naturally, although in many Western countries the ability is either latent or appears lost. The good news is that everybody should be able to access this ability and relearn the art of seeing auras. For some, the process may take longer than others but, ultimately, it is possible for anybody to see an aura. The aim of this book is to help you to do exactly that!

How to Use This Book

In the following chapters we'll take you through a series of exercises to enable you to begin seeing auras. It's important to take the steps at your own pace. Read through the whole of the book first, in order to get an overview of the process you'll need to implement but then return and take each stage step by step. Once you have completed the section to your satisfaction, move on to the next. Remember that seeing auras is perfectly possible for everyone but each of us takes our own time to do so. Be patient and persevere with steps and you'll be sure to be successful. The steps and techniques in this book are designed to be straightforward and simple for everybody to implement and should be easy to master in a relatively short time. Best of luck!

Chapter 2
Seeing Auras: Getting Started

Seeing auras seems to be an intrinsically human talent, yet many of us don't seem to have that talent "naturally". It's quite possible that as very small infants we do see or sense more than we do as we grow older. The "unfocused" way in which small babies seem to be viewing the world around them may be an example of this. We assume that their gaze is wide and broad because they are attempting to learn to view the world "correctly". Unfortunately, by the time we've taught them to speak, and can ask them what exactly they're looking at, we've also taught them a lot of other things, including what it's acceptable to say! Many parents may have been surprised at the answers very young children have come up with to a question like this, or may have dismissed comments about "lights" as pure fantasy. Some individuals may even vaguely remember a more colorful world in their toddler-hood than the world seems to be now, but be unable to accurately remember the details.

Either way, most of us have forgotten or lost the ability somewhere on the road, usually fairly early on, to becoming a responsible adult. Time to drop some of that responsible attitude and start taking some baby steps! In the first three of those steps we'll go through some basic methods to get your eyes accustomed to the world in a whole new light; a bright colorful one!

Seeing auras is visual trick; as discussed in the previous chapter it's possible, probable, that the color we see is simply a response triggered in the brain to our a physical reaction to subtle perceptions of the energy around all objects. Teaching your brain to see "more" than is actually there is simply done by training your eye to see the aura around a color. Training to see the human aura is more complex and difficult but seeing the aura of color is straightforward as the aura around bold colors is much more visible than that around the body. In these first steps learning to see auras around color is the primary aim.

Step 1: Setting the Scene

Auras are not visible in the dark and for these exercises you'll need a well lit space, not too bright but certainly not dim. Soft light is ideal, so normal daylight, perhaps softened with thin blinds. To begin with try to practice these exercises in the daytime, as you gain experience you'll find it easier to see the aura in a range of light conditions but the brighter the better until you become more experienced.

Try to have the source of light behind you; so sit with your back to the windows if using natural daylight, or with the light stood behind you if using normal lighting. Ideally you should conduct these steps with an object that is placed against a white wall or surface; if neither are available use white paper or a sheet to create the effect if possible. Relaxing and concentrating at the same time is key to being able to see an aura; you need to learn to gaze but not look directly at the objects in front of you (think of that wide-eyed stare seen in young infants).

You'll need a suitable object of a single color to start your first exercise. A book (or book-sized) object is ideal. In terms of color you should choose red or blue; these are strong, primary colors and give off a very visible aura. The object should be one, block color so if it isn't use colored paper and wrap the object. Again a book is probably the easiest choice as it allows for neat folding giving clear expanses of color. Stand the object upright directly in front of your white wall approximately six feet from where you will be sitting or standing. The distance can vary from individual to individual but you should aim for a minimum of four feet.

Notes:

- Use primary colors only as the aura of the color will be affected by the tone or hue. Avoid patterned objects, paper and background.

- Any object can be used as long as it is a bright, primary color, although a book is an ideal size. For larger objects vary the distance you place the object from yourself and try to avoid smaller objects.

Step 2. Losing Focus and Staying Concentrated

Wear comfortable clothing and ensure the room temperature is neither too hot nor cold. Ensure you are in a position that is comfortable for you; you don't need to be in the lotus position (or any other exotic position) to complete the exercise, the couch will be fine. Settle yourself in a comfortable position at the right distance from the object. Close your eyes and take a few minutes to calm your breathing by taking slow, deliberate breaths. Inhale and exhale using your stomach, allowing your diaphragm to push air in and out of your lungs. After a moment establish a regular, deep breathing pattern at a rate that is comfortable for you. Once you feel a sense of calm enveloping you open your eyes and look towards the object. Don't focus on it but let your eyes gaze in the general direction, focusing on nothing in particular, as if you were gazing slightly to the side of the object at the wall but not focusing on that either. The aim of this step is to see the object out of your peripheral vision, just out of normal focus. Continue to breath in a relaxed manner and gaze at the object, hold the gaze but don't strain your eyes or facial muscles. Concentrate on the task but don't become tense. Your gaze should become fixed, concentrated and intense but not focused on any particular object.

Blinking

You'll soon feel the urge to blink and may resist doing so. However, if you don't blink your eyes will start to water, itch and burn, which will only distract you. As you practice this step learn to blink naturally without changing your level of focus. Under normal circumstances we blink all of the time without noticing and often re-focus as we do. In this step you need to learn to allow your body to continue to blink normally but not lose the focused gaze you are aiming to achieve. Once you have begun to see the aura, blinking may cause it to disappear momentarily but it will reappear. Don't become preoccupied with blinking but allow it to happen as naturally as possible. The key is to remain calm and continue to breathe in a relaxed way.

Opening the Third Eye or Brow Chakra

The ability to view an aura is linked in many traditions to the concept of the Third Eye, sometimes known as the Brow Chakra and believed to be related to the power of clairvoyance. This book does not seek to support or deny any spiritual tradition and the subject of the Third Eye is as complex and often as contentious as the subject of the aura. As the aim of the book is to teach you to see auras we'll leave you to research and explore that concept elsewhere! For the purposes of this book the following exercise has been found useful by many people in order to see auras. Many people argue that it is possible to see auras without opening or stimulating the Third Eye but it is certainly easier to achieve if you do so. Use the following technique to stimulate and open the brow chakra, as you do so remain in the same pose, breathing calmly and deeply.

- Remember and visualize a time when you felt exhausted. Imagine the feeling of not being able to keep your eyes open, and the feeling of having to fight to do so. The sensation is very like trying to fight off a dark veil falling across your vision. When you do try to open your eyes the muscles of your eye lids fight so hard that the exercise becomes almost purely mental.

- As you remember this feeling in detail experience that sensation of mental effort to keep your eyes open. Your two eyes should, during this exercise, remain open. The mental effort is designed to open that third, intuitive eye. Simply focus on the sensation as you remember it and concentrate hard on how it feels.

This technique may take a few minutes or longer but in most cases it will begin to bear results quickly. With your two eyes firmly open the mental exertion starts to operate on your Third Eye, forcing it to respond and focusing energy on that area of your body. You should soon begin to experience a tingling, warm sensation at the center of your forehead between your eyes. As it does so keep your eyes firmly concentrating but slightly unfocused on the object and allow the Auric vision to appear. Allow you sense of feeling and awareness to shift to the center of your brow as you practice this part of the exercise.

If you find that you are having difficulty in opening or sensing this Third Eye there are some additional steps you can try.

- First, as you practice the above steps, simply lightly scratch the center of your brow above the eyes.

- Physically lift your brow as you would if you were trying to force your eyelids open. Just using the muscles of your brow, force the area upward. Keep practicing this lifting action on and off for a few minutes. However, don't allow your brow to become tense, remain calm and relaxed. If you find tension is building, take a moment and simply continue to breath and stare in the direction of the object.

- Imagine a swirling motion in the area of the Third Eye; the swirling should be clockwise, from the inside, and simply alternate this with lifting exercise above.

Gradually a physical sensation will occur in the area of the Third Eye and as it does so continue to relax and stare towards the object. This part of the exercise can take minutes for some or much longer for others. However, it is a crucial part of the process and will attune your body to begin seeing auras. Once you have a sensation of the Third Eye, don't give up. You are now close to seeing your first Aura.

The First Aura

At this point the first glimpse of an aura will appear. This should take the form of a faint shimmering around the object. This is known as the etheric aura and is a pale, shimmering band that surrounds the object. Don't worry if this appears as just a pale, insubstantial light, as this is normal. If you blink during this part of the process the aura will disappear momentarily but it will return. Viewing this first part of the aura is exciting and the temptation will be to suddenly focus on it; don't!

Stay relaxed, calm and maintain the gaze and concentration and don't suddenly look directly at the aura. Gradually a much brighter aura will develop. If you are using a blue object this will appear as a bright yellow color or if you are using a bright red book it will appear as a green color. This aura will gradually form around the etheric aura of the object; during this stage it is important to stay calm and view the aura from your peripheral vision. If you blink or glance directly at it, the aura will disappear. It will reappear but this can take a few minutes; if this happens remain calm and wait patiently, gradually the aura will reappear.

In most cases, during this stage of the process the aura will appear and disappear regularly. Simply stay calm and focused and gradually it will become more stable.

Congratulations

You've seen your first aura! This is an important step and the next steps will be much easier to complete. However, before you move on to them it's important to continue to practice the above exercises as often as possible. Practice, as in so many areas of life, makes perfect! Use these exercises once a day, if possible, but several times a week as a minimum. Continue with the exercises for several weeks, depending on how successful you are and how well you are able to view the aura.

Once you are able to set up the above tools, settle comfortably and promptly see an aura you are well on the way. When the aura remains constant, rarely flickering out of view, your skills are well developed. Don't worry that occasional lapses in vision occur when viewing the aura. "More or less" constant is the key here, all auras both of simple color as in this exercise, and animal, plant and human auras, will fluctuate in your vision. For most people practicing these exercises three or four times a week for around one month will be enough to get them to a competent stage of aura visualization. In many cases you will begin to notice auras around other objects and some of these may be living objects. Don't focus on these too much but don't ignore them. Gradually they will become a familiar part of your life and in the next steps we'll explore them in more detail.

Chapter 3
The Next Steps; Broadening Your Skills

In this chapter the steps are much shorter; we'll cover them in the form of tips for viewing auras around more complex groups of objects and living objects. In practice you should employ the main exercises described in the previous chapter as you begin to explore this new, vibrant world. The key exercises are learning to relax, keep the object in your peripheral vision without looking directly and yet without losing concentration. In all of the following steps incorporate all of the techniques you have already learned as you practice them. If you have practiced the previous exercises carefully, over a few weeks, they should by now be second nature.

Step 3: Mixing Things Up

We're not quite done with objects or books yet; in the first exercise a single object was used to hone your skills. Living auras are complex and interwoven with energies around them. In order to learn to identify one aura from another this step involves gathering several objects together. Again, books are an ideal size and form to practice with but other objects can be used. Take several books or objects and wrap them in different colors. Again, primary colors are ideal but practice this step initially with primary and then add other colors into the mix. Begin with three objects and aim to add up to another three.

Firstly study each object individually and make a note of the aura colors you see. Then combine first two and then three objects. Now make a note of the individual colors you can discern and the shades and shapes they make as they overlap. Add a third object and do the same again. Mix the order of the colors and the placing of the objects. Stand them in a row, lay them on top of each other and scatter them. Each time make a note of how the auras appear and how they affect each other. Add more objects and continue to practice viewing multiple objects and their auras.

A good idea in this step can be to mix objects of different colors and different sizes, or even different shapes. Keep the shapes relatively simple at this stage but mix things up a bit to see how the different auras mingle, blend and clash. Although we are still only dealing with the auras of color here, it's a good exercise to train your vision to the complexities of the auras you'll experience with different types of aura.

As with the first exercise it is useful to continue with this for some time. The more practice you get the more expert you'll become. You should find that with time the appearance of the auras is rapid and stable and that you can soon identify the individual aura for an individual object amongst a rainbow of colors. This is the primary aim of this step.

Step 4: Your First Living Aura

Now for a living object! In this case a plant is ideal as they tend to be less mobile than animals or birds. Fresh cut flowers can be used but they may not be ideal for beginners as their vitality is fading, even if they are kept well-watered. Also it is useful to choose a plant of a single color in the early stages of this exercise, so a green leafy plant will be ideal. A pot plant is a better subject for beginners. Try to ensure that the specimen you choose is vibrant and healthy. The auric color of the plant is the most likely thing you will notice first, that is the aura generated by the color as you've viewed in the first steps. A green leafy plant will generate a color aura of a orange color; the green in plants is not a pure primary color so the aura will not be pure red. View this subtle color carefully for a while using all your skills of calm concentration. Gradually you will observe a much stronger shimmering effect in the aura, like the etheric aura around the objects you've used but much brighter. Allow this to develop in its own time and don't be disappointed if it fades in and out of vision for a moment or two. Gradually this will become increasingly vibrant and seem to pulse. The energy radiating from the plant will soon become visibly very obvious. Without staring directly at it take notes as to its appearance and any variations in the quality or strength of the aura.

When you have completed the session, look over your notes. If you've spotted weaker areas in the aura take a closer look at the corresponding areas on the plant itself. Are there any signs of weakness, illness or areas in need of attention? Any particularly strong areas in the aura may indicate budding flowers or new shoots. See how the aura you've noted corresponds to the plant itself.

You may also like to try mixing more than one plant together as you become more experienced. Try different species, different colors, those with flowers and those without. Mix the types together and observe the effects. You can add a plant that is in need of some tender love and care alongside a vibrant, healthy plant and observe the difference in auras.

Step 5 – Big Plants!

We're talking trees here, and if you don't already love these creatures you soon will after you have viewed their expressive, often huge, auras for yourself. Observing the aura of a tree, as with a plant, is easier than many other living objects as they tend to be relatively stationary (this doesn't apply to their auras, coincidentally, as you'll experience). It's important to choose the right tree to begin with and the right time of day. This has nothing to do with species but more to do with location. Remember you'll need to reach a stage of calm focus without being disturbed and this is less easy when out of doors than it is at home.

Find a quiet location where the chances of being disturbed are limited. Out in the country is ideal but parks and public spaces can be used. Wherever you choose think about your own safety; you don't want to be too isolated or put yourself in a vulnerable position. As you zone out of our normal state of consciousness into a deeper level of consciousness you may lose some awareness of what is going on around you. It may be ideal to start this step with a friend and while one of you observes the aura, the other can observe what is going on in the environment around you both.

Viewing times can affect the visibility of the aura. The best times are early in the day or later on close to sunset, when the sun is lower in the sky. Remember the light source should be behind you, so choose a location and time of day where this is possible to achieve. You also need to be a reasonable distance away from the tree in order to see the aura. The top of the tree should be visible to you from the point you choose; a good way to identify the right distance is to estimate the height of the tree and then multiply this by three; this will place you at about the correct distance to view the tree as a whole with the top clearly visible.

As long as you have practiced the previous steps and become competent at viewing auras, viewing the aura of a tree should be simple. Simply get yourself comfortable, relaxed and begin viewing the tree as you would the objects and plants in the previous exercises. The aura itself will be influenced by several factors; the color of the leaves, the bark and the surrounding terrain. The sky will also "wash" the aura with color, so on a clear day a it will have a touch of light blue or on a cloudy one a gray color.

The aura around a tree is often huge, depending on the size of the tree itself. In some cases it simply expands around the tree pulsing with light and in others will appear as a fountain, spraying out of the top and down around the tree. Unlike a simple color aura the tree's aura will be sparkling and flashing with light and energy; the pulse and strength of this can be infectious and you'll almost certainly feel drawn to the tree itself. Take time to calm yourself and continue to observe. You may lose sight of the aura on several occasions but this will soon return. Make some notes and some observations if you can, as to the state, appearance and vibrancy of the aura. When you've completed your observations you can explore the tree up close to check for any correspondences in its physical condition and its aura's appearance.

Step Six: Animal Magnetism

Moving on to living, moving creatures. Observing an animal is much the same as observing plants and objects with one fairly big and obvious difference. Animals like to move around and seem to love to do so if you need them to stay still. Domestic animals are, in general, a good starting point. Cats and dogs are perfect if you've access to one or the other. An older, but not too old, individual, particularly shortly after being fed and/or exercised is even better. "Sleepy" is the keyword here.

Etiquette; as you develop your ability with auras you'll almost certainly develop a heightened sense of respect for every living thing around you. When observing animals, be aware of your impact on them. To a cat, a direct stare is a challenge and a threat that is met with either attack or flight. Take time to let them relax, fall asleep and, as you can't normally pin them to a white wall or surface, try to create a comfortable area or two which just happen to be covered in white sheets. Use a few, as a cat will avoid the one you want if there's only one. Dogs too can find direct stares aggressive but they can at least be easier to direct to your white-sheeted area of choice.

Practice your breathing exercises while the animal practices getting settled and having a nap, then start to observe them. If you are using another type of animal consider the advice in this paragraph and adapt as necessary!

The process is the same as described in the initial steps but it should now come naturally to you. Animal auras are not as bright as human but they are very distinct and often very clear. The color of the animal's coat will affect the uric color but you'll rapidly discern the bright, energy aura around the creature. Quietly observe this and again, note any changes in the quality or color of the aura. As with plants, areas in need of treatment can be identified with animal's aura.

Step 7: The Big One

Now it's time to start actively viewing the human aura. You may, almost certainly will, by now have started to notice them in some form or another as you work through the previous steps. However, human auras are complex, subtle and should be left until last in your steps towards viewing auras.

The best place to start when observing human auras is with your own! In this case you won't be able to observe your whole aura but you can simply use part of your body. With a plain white background, use your arm or legs to start. Use exactly the same techniques as described in the first steps of the book and take your time. The human aura is bright, multi-colored and vibrant. In a healthy individual it appears as a rainbow of color completely surrounding them. Dark patches or dull patches indicated areas of low energy which can indicate ill health or low mood in some way.

At first allow yourself time to simply view your own aura and learn to be able to do so without the image flickering out of view too often. The previous steps should make this possible and relatively easy to achieve. The next step is to find a willing friend!

The Human Guinea Pig

Again the process is much the same as with the previous steps; a light neutral background is ideal. In this case, light neutral clothing is also recommended. White, beige or similar colors should be worn by the individual. Remember that bright colors will give off an Auric color of their own so should be avoided. Additionally, an individual's aura may be affected by their mood becoming fainter and less visible if they are low, tense or bored. Try to arrange a positive atmosphere for the exercise, make sure the temperature is comfortable, lighting good and get them to choose their favorite music, to help relax them.

The main point of the exercise is for you to sit and stare at someone for a reasonable period of time! This can be an uncomfortable experience for both of you! You need your subject to be relaxed and not to move around too much; reading is the perfect occupation in this case. TV or videos are OK but emotions may cause rapid fluctuations in their mood and excitement may cause them to jump around! Quiet, with music they like and a good book is an ideal setting. You can, of course, arrange this scenario without them knowing why, but once you've stared at them for a while in a gazing, entranced way they may get the wrong idea! Be honest with your subject is the best advice!

The colors in the human aura relate to different functions within the body and also in a spiritual sense. These colors are defined and described in many Eastern traditions and are related to the colors that these traditions ascribe to the Chakras, or energy centers in the body. These are defined briefly below but you can research them in more detail in books relating to the subject of Chakras and Energy Healing.

Color Correspondences

- **Red;** physical energy, vitality, stamina, grounding, spontaneity, passion.

- **Orange;** creativity, productivity, pleasure, optimism, enthusiasm, emotional expression and sociability

- **Yellow:** fun, humor, lightness of spirit, personal power, intellect, logic and creativity.

- **Green;** balance, harmony, love, communication, nature, creativity, practical ability and acceptance.

- **Blue;** calmness, peace, honesty, love, inner peace, devotion, spirituality and emotional depth.

- **Violet;** intuition, imagination, meditation, creativity and artistic qualities, balance of energy and connection to universal energy flow.

Finally

This is the final stage in your steps towards viewing auras! When you make it to this point, congratulations! Auras are amazing things in themselves but can allow you to not only view the world in a completely different way but also to gain a better understanding on the mood and health of those around you. Seeing auras can inspire a great awe in the wider world around us and is valuable skill in life. I hope that this book has helped you to take your first steps on the journey towards a greater sense of enlightenment and greater healing abilities in the world!

Conclusion

Thank you again for downloading this book!

I hope this book was able to help you to understand the steps you'll need to take to begin to see Auras for the first time.

The next step is to begin practicing the steps one by one. The majority of the hard work is in the first few steps and, once you have mastered these, you will find the next steps much easier. Take your time, practice hard and I wish you every success!

Finally, if you enjoyed this book, please take the time to share your thoughts and post a review on Amazon. It'd be greatly appreciated!

Thank you and good luck!

Preview of *Reiki for Beginners*

Learn About Chakras, Auras And Energy Flow Throughout Your Body!!

With a somewhat mystical reputation, there is much misunderstanding, confusion and misinformation about Reiki as a healing technique. To many it is a mysterious, eastern, unproven technique, while to others it's one of a range of traditional alternative methods of healing in which the focus on healing the whole body and the mind is given wider priority than on simply healing specific illnesses.

This book is designed for the absolute beginner - with chapters clearly laying out the fundamentals of this eastern practice.

Here Is A Sneak Peek Of What You'll Learn...

- An Introduction To Reiki
- Understanding Each Chakra
- Learning How To Feel Each Chakra
- Chakra Exercises
- Auras And Their Significance Learning How To See Auras
- The Path Of Reiki Practice
- Seeking out Reiki Mentors and more!

Check Out My Other Books

Below you'll find some of my other popular books that are popular on Amazon and Kindle as well. Simply click on the links below to check them out. Alternatively, you can visit my author page on Amazon to see other works done by me.

If the links do not work, for whatever reason, you can simply search for these titles on the Amazon website to find them.

http://www.amazon.com/Astrology-Complete-Perfect-Personality-Horoscope-ebook/dp/B00N6HWV6K

http://www.amazon.com/Chakras-Beginners-Understanding-Sprituality-Meditation-ebook/dp/B00LNC6YGS

http://www.amazon.com/Crystals-Ultimate-Crystal-Healing-Spirituality-ebook/dp/B00SWMDP46

http://www.amazon.com/Numerology-Ultimate-Uncovering-Creating-Horoscope-ebook/dp/B00O6HWE8O

About the Author

I want to thank you for giving me the opportunity to spend some time with you!

For the last 10 years of my life I have studied, practiced and shared my love of spirituality and internal development. I kept diaries for years documenting the incredible changes that graced my life. This passion for writing has blossomed into a new chapter in my life where publishing books has become a full time career.

I feel extremely blessed and fortunate to have the opportunity to share my message with you! Each of my books is written to inspire others to explore the many aspects of their internal world. My goal is to touch the lives of others in a positive way and hopefully be the catalyst of positive change in this world :)

I am forever grateful for your support and I know you will get immense value through my books. I am really looking forward to serve you and give you great insight into my passions!

Your Friend,

Mia Rose

Printed in Poland
by Amazon Fulfillment
Poland Sp. z o.o., Wrocław